A Thirty Day Devotional

THE POWER OF PRAYER

I0088275

Olivia Ellen Eder

THE POWER OF PRAYER
Copyright © 2022 by Olivia Ellen Eder

All rights reserved. Neither this publication nor any part of this publication may be reproduced or transmitted in any form or by any means, electronic or mechanical, including photocopying, recording or any information storage and retrieval system, without permission in writing from the author.

Scripture taken from the New King James Version®, Copyright © 1982 by Thomas Nelson, Inc. Used by permission. All rights reserved.

Print ISBN: 978-1-4866-2252-8
eBook ISBN: 978-1-4866-2253-5

Word Alive Press
119 De Baets Street, Winnipeg, MB R2J 3R9
www.wordalivepress.ca

WORD ALIVE
—P R E S S—

Cataloguing in Publication may be obtained through Library and Archives Canada

*I would like to dedicate this book first to God,
who laid it on my heart to write a devotional on prayer.*

*I would also like to dedicate it to the biggest
examples of being a prayer warrior in my life:
Grandma Eder and Grandma Webster.
May God bless and keep you both!*

Acknowledgements

I would like to thank the team at Word Alive Press for all their willingness and kindness in helping me complete my devotional. I also would like to thank my family and friends that have encouraged and supported me in my endeavour to write a second book.

Contents

Fear

Day One

Reading: Matthew 10:28-31

"And do not fear those who kill the body but cannot kill the soul. But rather fear Him who is able to destroy both soul and body in hell. Are not two sparrows sold for a copper coin? And not one of them falls to the ground apart from your Father's will. But the very hairs of your head are all numbered. Do not fear therefore; you are of more value than many sparrows."

Fear controls us, doesn't it? In our lifetime, there are many things that can scare us. Think about it. From the time we are born, fear is always there because of the fall (Genesis 3). However, God commands us not to be afraid (Matthew 10:31), but to trust Him.

Pretty simple to do, right? Well, it can be, but not always. There are times when fear can control us in unexpected situations. For example, a loved one could have a serious illness. Even though fear is all around us, we shouldn't be conformed to its hold, but be transformed by the renewing of our minds (Romans 12:2).

There are two kinds of fear. One is a paralyzing fear and the other is a respectful fear. For example, we fear God because He has the power and authority over us. Whatever fears we have, we can conquer our fears by looking to the Rock of our salvation!

What are you afraid of? How can you be a conqueror instead of living in defeat?

Love and Hope

Day Two

Reading: Romans 5:1–5

"Therefore, having been justified by faith, we have peace with God
  through our Lord Jesus Christ, through whom also we have access
  by faith into this grace in which we stand, and rejoice in hope of the
  glory of God. And not only that, but we also glory in tribulations,
  knowing that tribulation produces perseverance; and perseverance,
  character; and character, hope. Now hope does not disappoint, be-
  cause the love of God has been poured out in our hearts by the Holy
  Spirit who was given to us."

Love. What is it? The world thinks love is like lust, but it's not true. Far from it. In fact, Paul makes it clear what love should look like. He gives a list of ten points in 1 Corinthians 13:4–7. However, I'm going to emphasize three. First of all, true love means that we have to show patience. "Love suffers long and is kind" (v. 4). Of course, we've heard this verse before at weddings, but do we take the time to understand what it really means? What does it mean to be kind? Maybe opening a door for someone who can't do it on their own, or simply praying for them.

For me, showing love means showing patience. For example, I have a disability called cerebral palsy. I have had this since birth. This means I need physical assistance for all my care. I have an attendant come into my home, who also works as a "online

EA." It has not been easy sharing her. This is where God's grace and patience comes in!

Second, not only do I have to show love every day, but in order to show love, I have to show kindness. To be honest, sometimes I find this a challenge. There are some people in my life who get on my nerves. Even so, I know that if I want to be one of God's disciples, I have to practice kindness daily. Like I said, this is not an easy task, but with God, it's possible to do (Matthew 19:26).

Finally, I believe the best way to show love and hope is to pray for people. I have seen how God can soften a heart a little, such as the heart of one of my workers. I remember one morning when she came into my house crying. When I asked her what was wrong, she opened up and shared what was troubling her. I told her that I would be praying for her, and she appreciated that. By the end of the day, I was physically and emotionally exhausted because of all the listening that I did. So, every night before I go to sleep, I pray for her.

Despite my frustrations, I'm learning how to show her love regardless of my feelings. We must also show the love that God shown to us.

How have you shown love? Do you show love only when you feel like it, or every day?

Pray Without Ceasing

Day Three

Reading: 1 Thessalonians 5:12-18

"And we urge you, brethren, to recognize those who labor among you, and are over you in the Lord and admonish you, and to esteem them very highly in love for their work's sake. Be at peace among yourselves. Now we exhort you, brethren, warn those who are unruly, comfort the fainthearted, uphold the weak, be patient with all. See that no one renders evil for evil to anyone, but always pursue what is good both for yourselves and for all. Rejoice always, pray without ceasing, in everything give thanks; for this is the will of God in Christ Jesus for you."

Over the past year or so, the world experienced an enormous change. From having freedoms to being limited, our world turned upside down. I find that praying through my problems helps with my anxieties. For example, if I hear that the Church is suffering, I will pray compassionately for them. My heart aches when I see my pastor looking worn out and like he's about to quit. This is why I pray.

In fact, the apostle Paul urges us to pray and uphold each other. No matter what the situation, I'm learning that if I keep my eyes on the Lord, He will give me the strength I need.

How about you? What is your prayer life like? I promise God will never fail you. We can trust Him!

What to Do with Unanswered Prayers

Day Four

Reading: Matthew 6:9–13

"In this manner, therefore, pray:
Our Father in heaven,
Hallowed be Your name.
Your kingdom come.
Your will be done
On earth as it is in heaven.
Give us this day our daily bread.
And forgive us our debts,
As we forgive our debtors.
And do not lead us into temptation,
But deliver us from the evil one.
For Yours is the kingdom and the power and the glory forever.
Amen."

Sometimes God will choose not to answer our prayers. However, that doesn't mean He's not listening or doesn't know the answers.

For example, I remember listening to a pastor on TV. When I was a baby, my mother found him while she stayed at home to take care of me. I don't remember what the sermon was about, but I remember this phrase that he used. He said, "Sometimes the answer is no, sometimes the answer is go, and sometimes the answer is slow."

I'm not sure why that phrase stuck, but it helped me through some challenging times. I think everybody should have that faith and determination—including myself.

Have you ever wondered why God is slow to hear? Is He even listening? We may not understand His ways, but we have to be obedient!

How Should We Pray?

Day Five

Read: Matthew 6:9-13

"In this manner, therefore, pray:
Our Father in heaven,
Hallowed be Your name.
Your kingdom come.
Your will be done
On earth as it is in heaven.
Give us this day our daily bread.
And forgive us our debts,
As we forgive our debtors.
And do not lead us into temptation,
But deliver us from the evil one.
For Yours is the kingdom and the power and the glory forever.
Amen."

Last time we talked about how we handle it if God chooses not to answer our prayers. I would like to move forward to explain how and what your prayer life should look like. Mind you, I'm not saying that you must do these steps in order for God to hear you. I just want to share with you what I find helpful when I pray.

First of all, I start with thanksgiving. I thank God for the good day that I had and for who He is. Second, I pray for my family, my church family, and my friends. Finally, I pray that God will use my writing in any way He chooses.

God answers in His own time and way. He always gives me strength to get through the day and beyond. Of course, I add that if God could grant my wish that I could have a boyfriend who loves Him as much as I do, I'll forever be grateful and will keep Him in the centre of the relationship. Even if He doesn't answer, I still say, "Thy will be done."

In your life, are you submitting to the will of God or to your own?

Have Faith

Day Six

Read: Matthew 8:26

"But He said to them, 'Why are you fearful, O you of little faith?'
Then He arose and rebuked the winds and the sea, and there was
a great calm."

Did you know that our lack of faith can hinder God from moving in our lives? As you read through the gospels, you will see that sometimes Jesus was amazed with people's faith, and sometimes very disappointed—especially with His disciples. Over and over again, we see Jesus reminding them to have more faith.

I believe He means to tell us the same thing. In my own prayer time, sometimes I've asked God to give me more faith. It certainly has been a long journey. There are many, many examples of how God answered my prayers.

For instance, I remember when I was almost done high school and was trying to decide which college I should go to. I toured different colleges around the area. One day, I took a tour at a college called Heritage College and Seminary. When I wheeled inside, I just knew it was the place God wanted me to be. Of course, I took it to God in prayer. I filled in the application forms and waited for a response. While I waited, I never stopped praying. True, I'd question if God really wanted me to go there. In the end, the acceptance letter confirmed it for me. I was so excited!

Now, I needed a support worker since the college couldn't provide one. Can you guess what happened next? Yep, you got it! I prayed and God answered. She was a Christian and we got along so well. The question for you today is: Do you have faith?

What are you believing? How can your prayer life be strengthened?

More than Conquerors

Day Seven

Reading: Philippians 4:13

"I can do all things through Christ who strengthens me."

In my opinion, we, as believers, shouldn't be living in defeat, but have power and confidence. Yes, our situation may seem hopeless, but God is so much bigger than our problems.

For me, since I have a physical disability called cerebral palsy, everything is a challenge. From the moment I was born, I have been through some unbelievable and remarkable things. For instance, when I was born, I was without oxygen for about a minute. All the doctors except for one thought for sure that this was going to be the end for me. Well, God proved them wrong! Because of His grace and my family and my church's prayers, I'm alive today! Philippians 4:13 is one of my personal favorite life verses. No matter what comes our way, we can have the victory—especially when we pray!

Have you ever said to yourself, "This is hopeless. I'm never going to get through..."? How can you have confidence in a God who will never fail you?

Why Should We Pray?

Day Eight

Reading: Hebrews 13:18–19

"Pray for us; for we are confident that we have a good conscience, in all things desiring to live honorably. But I especially urge you to do this, that I may be restored to you the sooner."

There are so many reasons why we should pray. Here are five reasons why I think it's important to do.

1. Prayer is a way to connect to God. Ever since Jesus died on the cross of Calvary, we have full access to call upon His name. Having a relationship with someone requires communication. This is no different with God. For me, it helps me to stay focused on Him when I pray. In order to grow in my relationship with God, I have to walk and talk with Him all day long. I set a time for us to talk. I have two times each day to do this. First, every day after breakfast, I do my devotions. I take about fifteen to twenty minutes each day to reflect on the Word and pray. Second, every night before I go to sleep, I pray that God would keep my family and my loved ones safe, especially during crazy times. Finally, I pray for God's will to be done in my life. For instance, God knows that my dream is to be a wife some sweet day. So, I ask Him for His direction in this.

2. Prayer gives us strength. I don't know about you, but I need strength every day—especially with my personal support workers. You see, most of my workers like to talk about themselves. This is the reason why I need God's strength and wisdom. I know that prayer is the key to any situation. So, I pray that He'll give me the wisdom and the strength to serve them.

3. Prayer connects us to God. I consider Him not only to be my best Friend, but my Father and my Redeemer. Since I can't hide anything from Him, I tell Him everything. Of course, He knows me and all of my thoughts. However, when I pray, God draws close—closer than a brother.

4. Prayer gives us direction. When I don't know what to do about something, I go to God in prayer, although I have to admit I like to work things out on my own. For example, if I have technology issues, I like to solve the problem by myself before I ask for help. Or during my school years, I remember struggling—specifically in math. I struggled with remembering all the steps for a mathematical question. I prayed hard, begging God to help me remember. He did and I got the highest marks!

5. Prayer is a weapon. Since the beginning of time, the devil is out there to kill and destroy (see 1 Peter 5:8). He hates it when believers pray, making him feel powerless and defeated. I know that there is power in the name of Jesus. As you can see, prayer is so important because God is so powerful and He cares about each one of us.

Do you really believe that God can answer your prayers? How much faith do you really have?

Be Obedient

Reading: Exodus 3:1-20

"So I will stretch out My hand and strike Egypt with all My wonders which I will do in its midst; and after that he will let you go." (v. 20)

When we pray, we are obedient to God. Throughout the scriptures, we see people being obedient through their prayers. From Abraham to John, we see God hearing people's cry and rescuing them. Usually, God gave them instructions on how to get out of their bondage.

One example is when the Israelites were captive in Egypt. For years, they cried out to God for mercy and help. Finally, He sent a man named Moses to help, although Moses had argued with God that he couldn't do it because of his poor speaking abilities (v. 11). Isn't it the same with us? We make excuses. However, God only asks us to trust and obey, because He knows the way!

Are you obedient to God's call? Ask Him to show you where you need to obey today!

Pray for Healing
Day Ten

Reading: John 14:13-18

"And whatever you ask in My name, that I will do, that the Father may be glorified in the Son." (v. 13)

In this passage, Jesus makes it clear that He loves it when we come to Him for help and answers. In fact, I believe this is why He came to earth: not only to save our souls, but to restore and heal us. Through prayer and faith, we can have the victory in our lives. If we seek Him first, He promises us that He'll answer our prayers.

When I was born, I was without oxygen for about a minute. My mom cried out to God and asked everybody at her church to pray for me. It was hard on both of my parents. My mom told God to have His way in both of our lives. He heard her prayer because she surrendered her will to His!

I believe that's the key. If we humble ourselves and surrender to Him, He will answer and give whatever we ask in His will.

Are you struggling with surrendering your will to God's? Ask Him to help you, and humble yourself before Him.

Wait on the Lord

Day Eleven

Reading: Isaiah 40:28-31

*"But those who wait on the Lord shall renew their strength; They shall
mount up with wings like eagles, They shall run and not be weary,
They shall walk and not faint." (v. 31)*

Waiting is hard, isn't it? For some, it's impossible. Others find
it a little easier to wait. Whether we have patience or not, God
expect His followers to wait on Him.

In this culture, everything is immediately available. I think
we've gotten used to it. I know I have. However, God call us to
be different than the world and to wait on Him.

Because I have a disability called cerebral palsy, I'm used
to waiting on others. There are days when I find it hard to wait,
though. For instance, when I have to go to the bathroom really, really badly, it's hard to wait for help. However, that doesn't
happen often because I've trained my body to go on a schedule.

It's similar with God. Like with my PSW, I have to wait on
Him and rely on His strength. There is good news though. God
is always on time!

What are you waiting for? How has God taught you to wait on Him?

Give Thanks
Day Twelve

Reading: 1 Thessalonians 5:16-18

"…in everything give thanks; for this is the will of God in Christ Jesus for you." (v. 18)

What does Paul mean when he writes, "In everything give thanks"? He means exactly that. We should thank God for everything He has done for us.

However, we sometimes forget and take Him for granted. I'm guilty of that as well. I mean, I try to be thankful, but I'm human. I forget. That's no excuse though.

I strongly believe that thankfulness should be a part of our prayer life. Remember how I told you previously about my prayer routine at night? I start my prayer with thanksgiving. This is like a child saying thank you to their parents. I thank God for His blessings, knowing that I don't deserve them. God is so gracious to us so, how can we not thank Him?

Are you thankful? Do you have a thankful heart?

Praying Together
Day Thirteen

Reading: Matthew 18:20

"For where two or three are gathered together in My name, I am there in the midst of them."

There is something powerful about praying with other believers, don't you agree? It can be a comfort knowing that someone has our back. It's fine to pray by ourselves, but we must remember we are a part of something bigger: a family! We shouldn't be living out our lives on our own. Instead, we should lift each other up in prayer.

In my own prayer time, I pray for my family and God's Church. Since I'm a member of God's body, I feel it's my responsibility to pray for them. I pray that God will keep His family safe and that we will be a light to the world. It's a comfort to know that I'm not alone and that there are others on the same road as I am. That's the point: we have to be there for each other, and together we are on our way Home.

Do you support your church by praying for them? Do they support you?

Pray for Your Enemies
Day Fourteen

Reading: Matthew 5:43–48

"You have heard that it was said, 'You shall love your neighbor and hate your enemy.' But I say to you, love your enemies, bless those who curse you, do good to those who hate you, and pray for those who spitefully use you and persecute you…" (v. 43–44)

In this passage, Jesus makes it very clear that He expects His followers to love their enemies. This is far beyond our nature, isn't it? At least, it is for me. To be truthful, I'd rather avoid people who are grumpy or unpleasant. However, God expects us to follow His example.

He goes further, saying that we should also pray for them (v. 44). I don't think that I have many "enemies," but there are people of whom I'm not a big fan. I try to be nice to them and ask God to help me to control my tongue. Sometimes it works, and sometimes I mess up and must ask for forgiveness.

I remember during my high school years, I had an EA that was mean to me. She accused me of not working hard enough. In the end, it was because I was a Christian and she didn't like that fact. Whenever I think about that time, I pray for her. It isn't easy, but I want to be an example of God's grace.

How about you? Who do you need to pray for? Remember, we were sinners too, saved by God's grace.

Trust God
Day Fifteen

Reading: Proverbs 3:5-6

"Trust in the Lord with all your heart; and lean not on your own understanding; in all your ways acknowledge Him, and He shall direct your paths."

After we've made our requests before God, He only ask us to do one thing: Trust Him! This is simple, and yet so hard to do. I have so many questions about my future. For example, is it God's plan for me to get married or stay single? I feel like God is just asking me to wait and trust Him.

As the proverb instructs us, we have to trust God with *all* of our hearts, and not just a part of them. I don't know why, but I find it hard to trust—not just with God, but with people too. Well, to be specific, young people. Because I have a disability and need consistent care, I find my friends are moving on without me. It's easy to make friends, but it's a challenge to keep them. However, I have to remember that God is not human and I can depend on Him to be there when I need Him. God is a good God, and He will never fail!

How can you trust God right now? Where is your faith? Keep believing, and I promise He will see you through.

God Knows Our Thoughts
Day Sixteen

Reading: Jeremiah 29:11-13

"For I know the thoughts that I think toward you, says the Lord, thoughts of peace and not of evil, to give you a future and a hope. Then you will call upon Me and go and pray to Me, and I will listen to you. And you will seek Me and find Me, when you search for Me with all your heart."

Did you know that God knows what we are going to say before the words come out of our mouth? I strongly believe we don't have to recite a certain prayer in order for God to hear us. Although we could, it isn't necessary because Jesus Christ is our mediator (see Hebrews 9:15).

We also have the Holy Spirit to translate for us because often we don't know what to say. God created us, and He knows us better then we know ourselves. This makes me humble because I know it's no use to hide anything from Him. For example, if I'm really concerned about someone or something and can't tell a soul, I usually give it to God in prayer. Even though we like to hide our troubles, let's be honest with ourselves and with God!

Who do you take your troubles to? Are you honest with yourself and God?

Asking for Prayer

Day Seventeen

Reading: Matthew 7:7–12

*"Ask, and it will be given to you; seek, and you will find; knock, and it
will be opened to you. For everyone who asks receives, and he who
seeks finds, and to him who knocks it will be opened. Or what man
is there among you who, if his son asks for bread, will give him a
stone? Or if he asks for a fish, will he give him a serpent? If you
then, being evil, know how to give good gifts to your children, how
much more will your Father who is in heaven give good things to
those who ask Him! Therefore, whatever you want men to do to
you, do also to them, for this is the Law and the Prophets."*

There is no shame in asking for prayer. In fact, God *wants* us
to ask. If you read through the scriptures, you'll see multiple
examples of people reaching out and God touching them. Since
we are His Church, it's our responsibility to hold each other up.

Sometimes I find it hard to ask for prayer. I'm a very private
person, and so I can't ask unless it's someone I trust. Otherwise, I
like to pray on my own, although I like to pray for someone else
whenever I'm in a small group or at Sunday services (quietly). I
believe this is why the Church is here, and we must do our part!

Do you have a hard time asking for somebody to pray for and with you? Is it because of pride or something else?

Give It to God

Day Eighteen

Reading: 1 Peter 5:1–7

"…casting all your care upon him; for he cares for you." (v. 7)

Most of us who have been saved for a while know that God's yoke is easy and His burden is light (Matthew 11:30). Unlike us, He never gets weary or tired. Peter instructs us to give everything we have to Him and leave nothing behind because He cares so much about us (v.7). For goodness' sake, He gave up his life just because He loves us! Also, He experienced life's trials while He was on earth, so He understands us. So what's holding us back?

When Jesus died on the cross, our sins and shame died with Him! What are you waiting for? Pray and lay your burdens down right now at Jesus' feet.

God Knows Best
Day Nineteen

Reading: Jonah 2:1-10

"Then Jonah prayed to the Lord his God from the fish's belly. And he said: 'I cried out to the Lord because of my affliction, and He answered me. Out of the belly of Sheol I cried, and You heard my voice.'" (v. 1–2)

Sometimes we think we know best. Unfortunately, we don't, and our pride gets in the way of really serving God. Jonah is a prime example of this. God told Jonah to go to Nineveh to preach about judgment and forgiveness. Of course, Jonah didn't think they deserved forgiveness because they were the meanest city around. After Jonah ran the other way and got swallowed by a great fish, he asked God to forgive him.

God did and Jonah got a second chance. Even though he still thought the Ninevites didn't deserve it, he went anyway. To Jonah's surprise, the people begged God for mercy, and He gave it to them.

In my life, I've doubted God's plan and trusted in my own way. Like Jonah, sometimes I want to control the situation and have my own way. This is where God intervenes and shows me my sins. At first, I hate the correction, but as I meditate and think about it, I know He is always right and looks out for my good. We can trust that God knows what He is doing, and be obedient to Him.

How about you? Do you really trust God? Do you want to follow God's plan or your own? Ask God for help today!

Access to the Throne

Day Twenty

Reading: Matthew 27:50–54

"Then, behold, the veil of the temple was torn in two from top to bottom; and the earth quaked, and the rocks were split…" (v. 51)

When Jesus died on the cross, a veil was torn from top to bottom. This means we have access to God's throne anytime we like. However, I strongly believe we must come to Him with fear and trembling.

Sometimes I think we forget that He is a holy God who deserves respect, honour, and praise. Yes, He is a loving God too. But because of sin, we can't have a deep relationship with Him— that is, until a sacrifice has been made. During the earthquake that occurred when Jesus cried "It is finished," a veil was torn in two. This means sin, death, and hell are no longer standing between God and us. We can have a free relationship with Him!

Do you know the kind of intimate relationship that I'm talking about? If not, will you ask God to help you today?

Praying for Direction
Day Twenty-One

Reading: 1 Samuel 15:10–34

"Now the word of the Lord came to Samuel, saying, 'I greatly regret that I have set up Saul as king, for he has turned back from following Me, and has not performed My commandments.' And it grieved Samuel; and he cried out to the Lord all night." (v. 10–11)

God wanted King Saul to let go of his reign. Saul was an evil king who wanted power and authority and always thought about himself. God felt sorry that He had even let Saul rule over Israel. The prophet Samuel had warned Saul many times that if he didn't smarten up, God would give the kingdom to someone else. Samuel prayed and waited for God's direction.

I think that's the key here. If we first ask God to give us direction as in what He wants us to do, everything else will fall into place. For example, I remember when I was looking for something to do after I graduated from Bible college. The first thing I did was pray. However, I had to do my part too. I researched jobs for persons with disabilities, and I found a place where I had received support when I was a child. I volunteered in the resource center once a week. Then I heard about a job fair at the college. I went to the fair and I saw a booth for a writing company. I was having issues with my power wheelchair at the time. It kept stopping and singing to me. The person at the booth thought I was interested because I was there for a while.

Little did I know this was what God had in store for me! The first thing I did was pray. I asked if this job was a part of His plan. God opened the door for me, and now I write articles for a Christian company called Power to Change. I love every minute of it! As you can see, if we ask for God's direction, He will show us His will for our lives.

Are you standing at a crossroad, not sure which path you should take? Stop for a moment and listen to what God is trying to say to you.

God Hears Us

Day Twenty-Two

Reading: Psalm 17:1–15

"Hear a just cause, O Lord, attend to my cry; give ear to my prayer which is not from deceitful lips." (v. 1)

In this Psalm, the psalmist is reminding God not to forget about him. God had been testing him to see if he was really following Him or if he was just going through the motions. Surprisingly, he passes the test and doesn't sin.

God really does hear our heart's cry. We may not understand what He is doing, but we can be assured that our prayers have been heard. When I think about all the prayers that I have prayed and how God has answered each one, I'm in awe of God's grace and love. True, He may not answer the way I think my prayers should be answered, but He always has an answer. The point is God does hear, and we can trust Him!

What are you asking God to do for you today? Remember that God is inclining His ear towards you, ready to listen.

What Is Prayer?
Day Twenty-Three

Reading: 1 Samuel 2:1–10

"And Hannah prayed and said: 'My heart rejoices in the Lord; my horn is exalted in the Lord. I smile at my enemies; because I rejoice in Your salvation.'" (v. 1)

Have you ever wondered what the point of praying is? You may feel like nobody is listening to you, right? The definition of prayer is: "a spiritual communion with God or an object of worship, as in supplication, thanksgiving, adoration, or confession."[1] In other words, it's talking with God.

In these verses, Hannah had just given birth to Samuel. Before Samuel was born, she prayed, pleading with God to give her a son. I'm sure she was grateful and somewhat shocked that a Holy God heard and answered her earnest prayer. In fact, she gave Samuel back to God, asking Him to have His way in Samuel's life.

I believe there's no correct way to pray. God knows our thoughts, after all (see Jeremiah 29:11–13). For me, I prefer praying aloud, especially at night, because it helps me focus on God. Sometimes my mind wanders, like a sailboat drifting on

---

1   https://www.dictionary.com/browse/prayer, accessed Jan. 24, 2022.

the lake. So praying aloud helps my prayer time with God. Everybody is different, so find out what works for you and do it!

What does your prayer life look like? How can you make it better?

Pray for the Authorities of the World
Day Twenty-Four

Reading: Matthew 17:17-22

"Then Jesus answered and said, 'O faithless and perverse generation, how long shall I be with you? How long shall I bear with you? Bring him here to Me." (v. 17)

There have probably been times when you've thought "What in the world is going on?" The world that you know is out of control: people hating each other and afraid of diseases.

I strongly believe prayer is the answer—for everything! If we, the people of God, are on our knees and praying, then God will do wonders and miracles. Time and again, I have seen God using tough situations for His glory. Although I'm young and still learning, I've realized that God really is good, and nothing surprises Him. If you read the scriptures, you know that God is the one who appoints people in leadership. I believe it's our job as believers to *pray* for those who are in charge, regardless how we feel. For me, I try to pray for the people in government, even though I'm not interested in politics. I trust that God is in control, so what are we doing?

Are you praying for God's mercy for your country? What can you pray specifically for your leaders today?

Praying for Internal Peace
Day Twenty-Five

Reading: John 14:23-31

"Peace I leave with you, My peace I give to you: not as the world gives do I give to you. **Let not your heart be troubled, neither let it be afraid.***" (v. 27)*

It's so hard to find peace in this crazy world, isn't it? If you look around you, you will see people worrying about getting a good job and making money. If they are young, they tend to worry about their spouse (or getting a spouse) and children.

Jesus promises a peace that surpasses understanding (see John 14:27). However, I believe we have to seek God's peace. For example, I get stressed and sometimes panicked when my parents don't tell me what their plans are or when technology fails me. This is when I must remember to turn to God and ask for His true peace. Of course, He always answers that prayer!

My point is, it doesn't matter if it's our job, family, school, relationships, or anything—we must remember to put our trust in the One who knows the beginning to the end, and rest in Him.

What are you worrying about? How can you have peace when the world around you is in chaos?

Pray for Forgiveness
Day Twenty-Six

Reading: Matthew 6:14–18

"But if you do not forgive men their trespasses, neither will your Father forgive your trespasses." (v. 15)

Everybody makes mistakes, right? Ever since the fall of man, we've fallen short of the glory of God (see Romans 3:23). However, God had a plan. He would end all sacrifices by making one big sacrifice: His only Son.

We now can ask for forgiveness and God won't condemn us! Not only that, we have the ability to extend forgiveness towards others because of what God has done for us. Although it's not always easy, this is what God commands us to do. Of course, God will help us and equip us to forgive.

Who do you need to forgive? What steps should you take to do this?

Pray for Contentment
Day Twenty-Seven

Reading: John 3:22–30

"John answered and said, 'A man can receive nothing unless it has been given to him from heaven.'" (v. 27)

What does it mean to be content? In this world, it's an impossible task. People are always complaining, and if we are not careful, we can let this become a habit ourselves. John the Baptist understood this. He could have been mad that Jesus stole his spotlight, but he chose to be content instead.

I don't know about you, but sometimes I have to ask God to help me be content. On the outside, I may look cool and collected, but on the inside sometimes it is not so. When I take my eyes off the Lord and look around me, I feel jealous. You see, most people my age are married and building a family of their own. Yes, there are some who are still single, but the numbers are getting lower and lower and lower! I'm really trying to be content in all things, though. God has given me blessings that I don't deserve. For example, my family, church family, and friends are all healthy. The point is that we must be content in whatever God has for us.

Are you content? What is God teaching you about contentment?

In His Time

Day Twenty-Eight

Reading: Psalm 69:1–11

"I am weary with my crying: my throat is dry; my eyes fail while I wait for my God." (v. 3)

God's timing is not our timing. Remember how in a previous devotion we talked about God knowing what's best for each of our lives? This is similar to what's happening in this passage. Read closely as to what the psalmist is trying to say here. He was drowning in sin, but God raised him up and forgave him. He trusted in God's way, not his own.

We must also be patient when we ask God for help (see Isaiah 40:31). I try to be patient. Sometimes I want God to answer my prayers on my timetable, but I know it doesn't work that way. I'm learning that God gives us just what we need at the right time! Trust in His timing and see what He can do.

Take a moment and think. Are you truly trusting in God or are you simply going through the motions? Remember, God's always there when we need Him!

Praise the Lord

Day Twenty-Nine

Reading: Psalm 150:1-6

*"Praise the Lord! Praise God in His sanctuary; Praise Him in His
    mighty firmament!*

*Praise Him for His mighty acts; Praise Him according to His excellent
    greatness!*

*Praise Him with the sound of the trumpet; Praise Him with the lute and
    harp! Praise Him with the timbrel and dance; Praise Him with
    stringed instruments and flutes! Praise Him with loud cymbals;
    Praise Him with crashing cymbals!*

Let everything that has breath praise the Lord.

Praise the Lord!"

One of the most important elements in our prayer life is to praise
God. David understood this. We can worship God in many different ways, including prayer. God doesn't care what method we
use because He cares about what's in our hearts. In fact, He's not
interested in big shows because He knows what's going on in our
lives and hearts.

I love to sing, and I grew up with music in my house. My
mom is the musician though. In her free time, she likes to play
the piano and sing. My favourite song is "Here I Am to Worship," written by Tim Hughes. Whenever I sing this song, I feel
the presence of God.

Do you praise God only when you feel like it? That's easy! What about when things aren't going your way and you are discouraged? This is the best time to praise the Lord and see what He will do for you!

The Faithfulness of God
Day Thirty

Reading: Psalm 89:1–13

"O Lord God of hosts, who is mighty like You, O Lord? Your faithfulness also surrounds You." (v. 8)

Do you ever feel like your prayers are floating around, not getting into anybody's ears? Eventually, you might give up because you think God isn't listening or doesn't care. Worse, you may feel like He has forgotten about you.

Let me reassure you that He hasn't! The psalmist knew this. He had experienced this firsthand. The Lord declared in verse 3 that He had made a covenant to remember him in time of need. He also promised that He would be with him through his trials.

This promise is for us as well. We may not get the whole picture, but He does! In my life, God has been faithful. He has provided for me in ways beyond my understanding. For example, I remember needing a new joystick for my wheelchair. It was getting old and was singing to me. I remember asking God to help it keep working till the new one came in. After what seemed like years, the new joystick finally arrived. The man who fixed it was shocked that the old joystick had worked for so long because it was all broken inside! I just smiled, knowing that God had kept His promise to me.

Just like He was with all the people in the Bible, God is true to His Word. From the time God promised Abraham that his seed would go on until now, He has been faithful and just to offer support and comfort to us. We can trust Him for everything because He is the same—yesterday and forever!

How has God been faithful to you? Can you really say with the psalmist in Psalm 89:1, "I will sing of the mercies of the Lord forever; with my mouth will I make known Your faithfulness to all generations"?

About the Author

Olivia Ellen Eder is the author of *A Miracle of God's Grace: My Life with Cerebral Palsy and My Journey with God*. This is her first devotional. She also writes articles for the organization Power to Change and has volunteered at KidsAbility Children's Centre. She is a graduate of Heritage College and Seminary. She loves children and has volunteered at many Christian camps as a counsellor and on the service team. Olivia loves music and enjoys singing at her church and with family and friends. She also has a passion to encourage and mentor others living with a disability or who struggle in any way. In her spare time, she loves to read a good Christian fiction novel. Olivia lives with her family in Waterloo, ON. You can contact her at ollieeder27@yahoo.com

www.ingramcontent.com/pod-product-compliance
Lightning Source LLC
Chambersburg PA
CBHW030154070426
42447CB00032B/1201

* 9 7 8 1 4 8 6 6 2 2 5 2 8 *